THE RAPTURE
Do Infants or unborn babies go to Heaven? When will the Rapture occur? Should a Christian be cremated?

RUSSIA
Why does Russia invade Israel? What is the sequence of events in the Russian invasion of Israel?

ANTICHRIST
Can my television set become a spy network for Antichrist? When will Antichrist be revealed? Will Antichrist be a resurrected individual? Who is Antichrist? Has a Mark system been devised?

THE TRIBULATION PERIOD
How will people be saved after the Rapture? How does the United States fit into Bible prophecy? What is meant by the 70 weeks of Daniel? Will the Tribulation take place immediately after the Rapture? Who will be saved during the Tribulation?

BATTLE OF ARMAGEDDON
What is the final alignment of nations? Does the Bible mention a time when all men will be saved?

JUDGMENTS
What are the four judgments? Will the Temple be rebuilt? Where are the unsaved dead before their Judgment Day?

MILLENNIUM
What is the difference between Resurrected and Living Believers? Will anyone be tempted by Satan in the Millennial Period?

NEW HEAVENS and NEW EARTH
Do those who have died know what is going on here on earth now? Will there be old and young in Heaven? Does a believer go to be with the Lord immediately after death? Will we be reunited with our loved ones in Heaven? Will we live again with our mates in Heaven?

All this and much much more you will find in the chapters of this exciting and revealing book that answers QUESTIONS MOST FREQUENTLY ASKED ON PROPHECY!

QUESTIONS
FREQUENTLY ASKED ME
ON PROPHECY
by SALEM KIRBAN

Completely Updated Revision. . . . . March, 1981

Published by SALEM KIRBAN, Inc., Kent Road, Huntingdon Valley, Pennsylvania 19006. Copyright © 1972, 1981 by Salem Kirban. Printed in the United States of America. All rights reserved, including the right to reproduce this book or portions thereof in any form.

Library of Congress Catalog Card No. 72-78025
ISBN 0-8024-7055-6

ACKNOWLEDGMENTS

To **Dr. Gary G. Cohen,** President of Clearwater Christian College, Clearwater, Florida, who carefully checked the final manuscript.

To **Doreen Frick,** who devoted many hours proofreading the text.

To **Estelle Bair Composition,** for excellent craftsmanship in setting the type.

To **Walter W. Slotilock,** Chapel Hill Litho, for negatives.

To **Koechel Designs,** for an excellent cover design.

CONTENTS

CHARTS

In Luke 18:15-17 infants were blessed by Christ. The Greek word here is **brephos,** the root from which we get the word *"brief."* It refers to babies and infants (and in Luke 1:41 to an unborn baby, yet in its mother's womb).

This blessing by Christ can neither be called accidental nor casual. Not that anything the Lord did could ever be called casual. An argument took place concerning it, and Christ went out of His way to make it clear to all that children should be brought to Him, *"for of such is the kingdom of Heaven."*

By the nature of the Greek word these were (or at least included infants) who clearly would not have even come close to approaching the age of personal decision. These infants in themselves could not have at this stage in their life personally accepted Christ . . . even in any Old Testament sense.

They were born sinners, still had the sinful nature. But their parents, apparently at the minimum, thought favorably of Christ. And perhaps it would not be too much to conclude, they probably accepted Him as the Messiah.

Christ's taking the children in His arms (from the other passages) . . . and blessing them here showed some type of approval or acceptance.

From this act, which we must take as significant of how God looks upon the infants of those who love His Son, I do not hesitate to conclude that:

1. We may safely place our trust in the fact that those who die in infancy who are the children of a believer, go to be with the Lord.
2. From 1 Corinthians 7:14, which declares the child of **one** believer to be *"clean"* (as opposed to the child where both parents are believers) . . . we take it that the above is true if **one** parent is a believer. This also fits with the fact of the Luke 2 incident, where we do not know that both parents of the infants blessed by Christ were present.
3. At the Rapture (1 Thessalonians 4:17), the infants of believers will be *"caught up"* along with their believing parent(s).

Many theologians, who are sound Biblical Protestants, have even argued that the infants and stillborn of even unbelievers go to Heaven. The Scriptural evidence is in this case not so clear.

I think that the reason the Bible does not make the point clear is that God wishes to give no encouragement for the unbeliever to remain in a state of unbelief. As far as we know, as long as the parents are in unbelief, the spiritual destiny of their children, should they die in infancy, is in jeopardy. Plus, most unbelievers have children who finally grow up to be unbelievers, unfortunately.

Dr. Gary G. Cohen

THREE VIEWS ON THE RAPTURE*

These are NOT millennial positions but merely three of the views on the exact time of Christ's return within the PRE-MILLENNIAL camp. Correctness on these positions have nothing to do with the salvation of a sinner.

THE RAPTURE POSITIONS	WHAT DOES IT MEAN	WHAT EACH GROUP BELIEVES	WHY MANY BELIEVERS HOLD TO THE PRE-TRIBULATION RAPTURE VIEW
POST TRIBULATION RAPTURE	The Church (believers) will be raptured AFTER the 7 year Tribulation Period.	The Church will go through the awful Tribulation. (Matthew 24:21).	The Church is to be spared God's wrath (Romans 9:5). Since the entire 7 year Tribulation Period is a pouring out of God's wrath (Revelation 6:17), the Rapture must remove the Church before this pouring occurs. Genesis 19:22 shows this principle. The angel could not begin to destroy Sodom until Lot was safely removed from the area!
MID TRIBULATION RAPTURE	The Church (believers) will be raptured in the midst of the 7 year Tribulation Period.	The Church will be saved only from the last 3½ year "Great Tribulation." (Matthew 24:21).	
PRE TRIBULATION RAPTURE	The Church (believers) will be raptured before the 7 year Tribulation Period starts.	The Church will be saved from the entire 7 year Tribulation. (Matthew 24:21).	

On the time of the RAPTURE, which is a complex topic, interested readers should refer to:
KEPT FROM THE HOUR, Gerald B. Stanton (Toronto: Evangelical Publishers, 1964);
THINGS TO COME, J. Dwight Pentecost (Grand Rapids, Michigan: Zondervan Publishing Company, 1958);
THE RAPTURE QUESTION, John F. Walvoord (Grand Rapids, Michigan: Zondervan Publishing Company, 1957);
UNDERSTANDING REVELATION, Gary G. Cohen, Executive Vice-President, Clearwater Christian College, Clearwater, Florida 33515).

*RAPTURE: This refers to the time when believing Christians (both dead and alive) will "In the twinkling of an eye" rise up to meet Christ in the air (I Thessalonians 4:13-18).

Chart by Dr. Gary G. Cohen

What is the Rapture?

This refers to the time, prior to the start of the 7 year Tribulation Period, when believing Christians (both dead and alive) will *"in the twinkling of an eye"* be caught up ("raptured") to meet Christ in the air. **The Second Coming of Christ** is one of the most prominent doctrines in the Bible. In the New Testament alone it is referred to over 300 times. His First Coming was over 1900 years ago when He came on earth to save man from sin.

The Second Coming is an event starting at the Rapture and comprehending four phases:

First, at the Rapture Christ takes the believers out of this world to be with Him (1 Thessalonians 4).

Second, Christ pours out His judgments on the world during the 7 year Tribulation Period.

Third, Christ at the end of the 7 year Tribulation destroys the Antichrist and his wicked followers (Revelation 19).

Fourth, Christ sets up His Millennial Kingdom prophesied so often in the Old Testament.

When will it occur?

Matthew 24:34, Mark 13:28-31 and Luke 21:29-33 and Luke 21:24 may well indicate that the Rapture Countdown begins when the time of the Gentiles ends. Whether a countdown can be con- sidered as starting in 1948 or 1967 or some other date is a matter of opinion. Even, however, if 1948 were an accept- able date . . . one cannot use the phrase of Matthew 24:34 *"This generation . . ."* and state that this means 30 or 33 years. This verse rather teaches that . . . those living in that time will not die until they see these things come to a final consum- mation.

SHOULD A CHRISTIAN BE CREMATED?

Cremation is the burning of a dead body. There is no verse in Scripture that absolutely forbids cremation. Most Christians, in fact almost all, allow or request for regular burial and avoid cremation. The reasons for this are generally as follows:

1. Burial is the method which is given as our example in both the Old and New Testaments. Joseph was buried; Moses was buried; and our blessed Lord was, on his crucifixion's close, buried.

2. There is no example of cremation among the saints in the Bible, in either Old or New Testaments.

3. The Bible in numerous verses speaks of our resurrection (Revelation 20:5, etc.). This refers to a giving of life again to the body. So too does 1 Thessalonians 4:16. 1 Corinthians speaks of the resurrection of the believing dead from the "grave." This presumes that the believers have a grave, and hence were indeed buried.

4. It thus, from the above, has been concluded by most Christians that burial, not cremation, is proper as it gives a testimony of our faith that God will indeed raise the dead.

5. Hindus and others, who do not believe in the resurrection of the saints by Christ, cremate without such concerns.

6. Revelation 20:13 says, "And the sea gave up her dead," and show that God, nevertheless, has the power to reconstitute and reconstruct, and reawaken a body scattered into the sea and probably devoured and digested by many fish (here speaking of the Great White Throne Judgment).

7. Some saints have been martyred to the flames and oceans, but we doubt not that they will be among the resurrection saints, yea, chiefest amongst them. Thus God can also in like manner resurrect a cremated saint, and indeed He will do it.

8. Thus, for reasons of example and testimony (i.e., the example of the Biblical saints and our testimony to those whom we leave behind), Christians bury and do not cremate. Cremation is not specifically forbidden and a saint could do it. I, however, for the above reasons, would not advise it.

Dr. Gary G. Cohen, President
Clearwater Christian College

Are Earthquakes A Sign Of The End Times?

Earthquakes are occurring in Tokyo very frequently . . . strong enough to set high buildings creaking on their girders. Continual earth tremors in Tokyo stir a big fear that a destructive earthquake is due. That is why . . . beginning one year ago . . . undertakers began storing collapsable coffins. Their goal: to produce 200,000 such coffins in anticipation of the big quake!

The Japanese remember the big quake in 1923 when some 100,000 died and 50,000 were missing. NOW . . . this same region in Tokyo has one-quarter of Japan's 117 million people. They are crowded into what is considered the most densely populated urban concentration in the world!

This year could be the year of many catastrophes . . . one may be the Tokyo earthquake that leaves thousands dead!

Collapsible coffins now being stored in Tokyo warehouse.

Matthew 24:7 tells us that one sign of the Last Days is: *". . . earthquakes in various places."* More and more we are reading about disastrous earthquakes occurring killing thousands, making many more thousands homeless.

What you may not realize is that GOD SPEAKS TO US through earthquakes but we don't listen! An earthquake generated the Mount St. Helens volcanic eruptions!

Look at these verses:

In Judges 5:4,5 . . . the Lord spoke to Israel through earthquakes and volcanic eruptions.

In Deuteronomy 33:2 . . . He brought ten thousands of His saints to witness this action.

In Psalm 68:17 . . . is a reaffirmation of the angels plus His chariots!

In Daniel 7:9, 10 . . . describes the battle of Armageddon and reveals that the angels who witness this event number into the MILLIONS!

Earthquakes and volcanic eruptions are not simply freaks of nature. They are *warnings from God!* Some 97 years ago, a volcanic eruption in Indonesia killed 37,000 people. But more significant . . . for a year after the eruption, sunlight reaching the earth was reduced 13%. The sun will also be darkened at the 4th Trumpet judgement in the Tribulation Period.

When Will The Dead Sea Flow Into The Mediterranean Sea?

Now! For the first time ever . . . PROPHECY IS RAPIDLY HEADING TOWARDS FULFILLMENT IN ISRAEL!

Let's get some background. In 536 BC some 50,000 Jewish exiles had returned to Jerusalem from Babylon. This was after 70 years in captivity.

Sixteen years later (in 520 BC), Darius 1, the Great, was King of Babylon. It was at this time that the prophet Zechariah had 8 night visions regarding events that would take place in the 1000 year Millennium.

Then TWO YEARS LATER in 518 BC, Zechariah made an astounding prophecy . . . a prophecy that seemed utterly impossible ever to reach fulfillment!

That was 2498 years ago! in 518 BC. Now . . . suddenly on August 24, 1980, this prophecy is rapidly moving towards fulfillment!

On August 24, 1980, the Israeli government approved the construction of a canal connecting the Mediterranean Sea with the Dead Sea! This was a project dreamed by the Zionist pioneers in the 19th century. But, more important it was a prophecy made by Zechariah almost 2500 years ago! *And yet we have people today who believe the Bible is a myth and man descended from a monkey. These are the same doubters who believe in the "big bang" theory and refuse to believe the Genesis account of creation!*

This proposed $700 million waterway is vital to Israel's energy needs! Water will tumble

through a 70 mile canal from the
Mediterranean Sea to the Dead Sea. The
Dead Sea lies 1300 feet below sea level. The
canal's pathway was unanimously approved
by the Israeli cabinet! But it poses some
delicate international problems. The Dead
Sea is mutually owned by Israel and Jordan.
And Jordan refuses to cooperate.

The money for the canal will come from
both public and private sources. Several
foreign investors are interested. The canal
will be some 50 feet wide and will run
through a tunnel for 55 of its 70 miles!

Critics of the canal have charged that
Mediterranean water spilling into the Dead
Sea may damage the Dead Sea's ecology.
Others have worried about the impact that

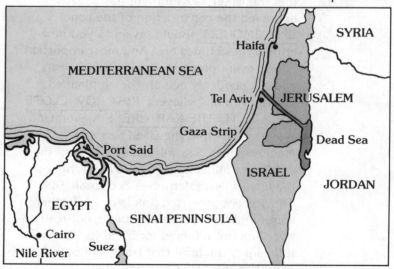

U.S.A. Copyright © 1981 by Salem Kirban.

While the Israeli government is planning a Dead Sea link with the
Mediterranean Sea . . . that actual waterway through Jerusalem will not
occur until the Millennium. See Zechariah 14:4,8.

raising the sea's level by almost 30 feet will have on Jordanian potash works on its East bank!

What Does This Mean?

Potash is an important element in making ammunition! Because there is no outflow in the Dead Sea it has become the world's most important source not only for potash but a host of other highly valuable minerals! No one really knows how much wealth is in the Dead Sea . . . as it is NOW! By allowing the Mediterranean Sea to link with it will destroy these mineral properties! *The very thought of this happening will greatly disturb Russia!* This very action (a move towards a Mediterranean-Dead Sea link) will cause Russia to MOVE UP her invasion plans of Israel . . . ahead of schedule. The very fact that the Israeli Government has already approved the construction of the canal UNANIMOUSLY should reveal to you how critical these times are! And most important . . . an event prophesied some 2500 years ago . . . suddenly actually being planned, indicates to all believers JUST HOW CLOSE WE ARE TO THE RAPTURE! However, God's Word tells us that the Dead Sea and Mediterranean Sea will not merge until the 1000 year Millennium. This will be through the city of Jerusalem. See Zechariah 14:8. The present proposed link is much further south in the Negev desert and is not really a river link but a tunnel for 55 of its 70 miles. It is highly doubtful that Israel will be able to complete this Dead Sea link plan!

**Why Does
Russia Invade
Israel?**

Either at sometime **prior to the Rapture** of believers or **during the first 3½ years** of the 7-year Tribulation Period, Russia will take an interest in Israel's wealth.

Why would Russia want Israel?

Perhaps the great prize which Russia wants is the vast mineral deposits in the Dead Sea. The Dead Sea is 1286 feet below sea level, the lowest spot on the surface of the earth! It is 50 miles long and nine miles wide. It is still known as the "Sea of Salt" because it is filled with salt due to its having no outlet. Fed chiefly by the Jordan River, its waters have evaporated for thousands of years in the fiery heat, leaving behind an ever-growing residue of salt and other valuable minerals. It is calculated that there is enough potash in the Dead Sea to provide the needs of the entire world for 2000 years!

With a growing famine in the world, potash becomes extremely important since it is used as fertilizer. Vegetation, and consequently animal life including human life desperately require it!

Russia wants potash in Dead Sea to make explosives!

But potash also has another use; that is in the making of explosives.

Russia—the Union of Soviet Socialist Republics—in area the largest country in the world—stretches across two continents from the North Pacific to the Baltic Sea. It occupies 1/6th of the earth's land surface.

So Russia, with her allies, will according to the Scriptures someday invade Israel (Ezekiel 38:1–39:16). At this time, because of Russia's march against the comparatively defenseless Jews, God's wrath is kindled:

> And it shall come to pass at the same time when Gog shall come against the land of Israel, saith the Lord Jehovah, that My wrath shall come up into My nostrils.
> (Ezekiel 38:18)

How Does This War Begin?

Russia will back the Arabs' claim to Palestine (Ezekiel 38).

Because the Antichrist will make a pledge to protect Israel the Jews will no doubt flock back to Israel in unprecedented numbers.

The Scriptures seem to give us some indication that in this time Russia may part with her Jews and allow them to return to Israel. It is estimated that there are over 2 million Jews in Russia at present.

After this occurs, Russia, feeling she is all powerful, will probably make her move into the land of Israel.

God will allow this to happen perhaps because His people are looking to the Antichrist as their saviour. Antichrist,

CRESCENT OF CONQUEST

RUSSIA'S GRAND DESIGN FOR MIDDLE EAST CONQUEST

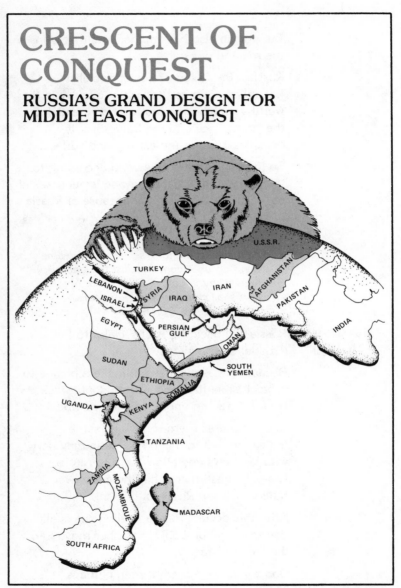

however, will turn on them. Therefore, the Jews will again be driven out of their land and many will flee from Israel and the two thirds of those left behind will be slain so that, alas, the soil of Israel will again be drenched with the blood of the children of Abraham.

> And it shall come to pass, that in all the land, saith the Lord, two parts therein shall be cut off and die; but the third shall be left therein (Zechariah 13:8).

> And among these nations shalt thou find no ease, neither shall the sole of thy foot have rest; but the Lord shall give thee there a trembling heart, and failing of eyes, and sorrow of mind: (65)

> And thy life shall hang in doubt before thee; and thou shalt fear day and night and shalt have none assurance of thy life: (66)

> In the morning thou shalt say, Would God it were even! and at even thou shalt say, Would God it were morning! for the fear of thine heart wherewith thou shalt fear, and for the sight of thine eyes which thou shalt see (67) (Deuteronomy 28:65–67).

After this occurs may be the time when God will step in and devastate Russia and Russian Communism, including her allies as He has prophesied in Ezekiel 38:1–39:16.

It seems that this is the time that the Federated States of Russia will take the Arabs' claim to Palestine (Ezekiel 38).

This may be the time that the Federated States of Europe will move into this vacuum created by the defeat of Russia. It is at this time that Antichrist will rule over all the earth.

Israeli women lay barb wire in preparation for coming invasion.

What is the Sequence of Events in the Russian Invasion of Israel?

The invasion of Palestine by Russia and her allies (The Northern confederacy) will bring Antichrist and his armies to the defense of Israel as her would-be protector.

Daniel 11:40-45 describes this invastion. The following is a suggested order of events:

1. The campaign begins when Egypt and her allies (The Arab confederacy), move against United Europe and Antichrist.

2. The Arab confederacy is joined by Russia and her allies (The Northern confederacy). Together they attack Jerusalem coming by land and sea. (Perhaps Jerusalem will be Antichrist's headquarters in the Middle East.)

3. Jerusalem is destroyed as a result of this attack (Zechariah 12:2). But the armies of The Northern confederacy are also destroyed (Ezekiel 38 and 39; Zechariah 12:4).

4. The full armies of Antichrist move into Palestine (Daniel 11:41) and conquer all that territory (Daniel 11:41–42). However, Edom, Moab and Ammon will escape the tyrannical rule of Antichrist (Daniel 11:41). These areas are now in present day Jordan, and Petra is in the Edom section of Jordan.

What Happens to Russia

The heavens will open and God will pour out a judgment from heaven that will wipe out the Russian military might and much of the power of the Russian confederacy.

What judgments are they?

There will be a severe earthquake and the earth around Israel will tremble severely. This earthquake will throw the soldiers into such a panic that in confusion they will kill one another.

> . . . the mountains will be thrown down . . .
> every wall will fall to the ground.
> Every man's sword will be against his
> brother.
> (Ezekiel 38:20–21)

In addition to this, sudden calamities will strike them and very violent rain and hail will fall down on them. And if this were not enough—fire and brimstone will explode right in their very midst. See Ezekiel 38:22.

Through this righteous indignation of God, we will find that the Russian armies with their allies will be destroyed without even being attacked by any other nations. All but one-sixth of the army will be killed!
See Ezekiel 39:2.

What is the extent of this vast judgment?

> Then those who inhabit the cities of Israel
> will go out, and make fires with the weapons
> and burn them, both shields and bucklers,
> bows and arrows, war clubs and spears and
> for seven years, they will make fires of them
> . . . For seven months the house of Israel
> will be burying them . . . Even all the people
> of the land will bury them.
> (Ezekiel 39:9, 12, 13)

It takes 7 years to burn and destroy weapons and 7 months to bury the dead. So great are the casualties that it takes all of the people of Israel to help in this great task!

With this destruction of much of the Russian power, a power vacuum is created. And Antichrist rushes in to close this vacuum!

In attempting to settle the Arab-Israeli dispute, he will side with Israel and back her claim to the land of Palestine against Russia.

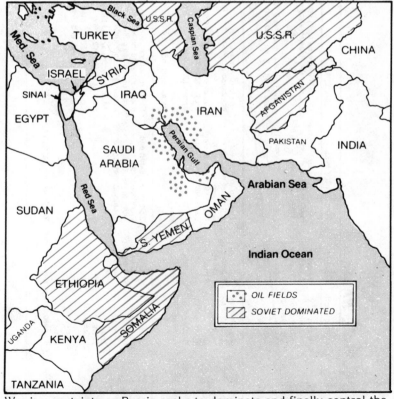

War is a certainty as Russia seeks to dominate and finally control the entire Middle East. It will be her downfall!

3 DECISIVE WARS

War	Participants	Occurs	Reason for War	Outcome	Scripture References
1	Russia and Allies (Arab nations, Iran, Germany) vs. Israel	Before or during first 3½ years of Tribulation Period *(This could happen at any time!)*	Possibly because Russia desires Israel's vast mineral wealth.	God will intervene and through an earthquake in Israel plus rain and hail, the Russian army will be wiped out. It will take the Israelites 7 years to collect the debris. It will also take them 7 months to bury the dead!	Ezekiel 38:1-39:16
2	**Armies from All Nations** vs. God at Jerusalem **Battle of Armageddon**	At End of 7 year Tribulation Period	Flushed with power Antichrist will defy God, seek to destroy the 144,000 witnessing Jews and Jerusalem.	The Lord Jesus Christ comes down from heaven and wipes out the combined armies of more than 200 million men. The blood bath covers over 185 miles of Israel and is "even unto the horse bridles." **(Revelation 14:20)** Antichrist and the False Prophet are cast alive into the Lake of Fire. **(Revelation 19:20)** Satan is bound in the bottomless pit for 1000 years. **(Revelation 20:1-3)**	Joel 3:9, 12 Zechariah 14:1-4 Revelation 16:13-16 Revelation 19:11-21 Ezekiel 39:17-29
3	Satan vs. God **The FINAL REBELLION**	At End of 1000 year Millennium Period	God allows Satan one more opportunity on earth to preach his deceiving message.	Satan will be successful in deceiving vast multitudes (out of those born during the millennial period) to turn away from Christ. This horde of perhaps millions of people will completely circle the Believers in Jerusalem in a state of siege. When this occurs, God brings FIRE down from Heaven killing the millions in Satan's Army. Satan is then cast into the Lake of Fire, where the False Prophet and Antichrist are, and they will be tormented day and night for ever and ever.	Revelation 20:7-10

Can My Television Set Become A Spy Network For Antichrist?

Very shortly . . . you will not be safe . . . EVEN IN YOUR OWN HOME! There is a big push to install cable TV in every home in America!

There are several reasons:

1. MONEY

   Cable TV is big business. One cable TV company stands to make 100 MILLION in just 15 years! Millions of dollars are at stake. It is a lucrative new business.

2. A LAUNDERING OPPORTUNITY

   Opportunities to make money attract underworld characters. Cable TV projects initially can cost $10 to $60 Million to start. Crime syndicates who have made millions on gambling, prostitution, etc. need to *"launder"* or channel this dirty money through a clean business. Cable TV offers this opportunity!

Cable TV has its advantages. You receive a clear picture all the time. There is no outside interference since a cable is run from an outside power line directly into your home and connected to your Television set! The largest cable-television franchise yet awarded will provide cable TV for 400,000 homes in Dallas, Texas. This system in Dallas will take 5 years to complete. It will cost an estimated $100 Million initially. *And here is the next advantage of cable TV* . . . it will offer subscribers up to 80 different channels to select from daily!

But What Are The Far-Reaching Possible Consequences?

Right now . . . 1 out of 5 homes with TV sets have cable television. The cable running into your home is connected to your TV. <u>This electronic system can provide an excellent way for the soon-coming ANTICHRIST to intrude on your privacy!</u>

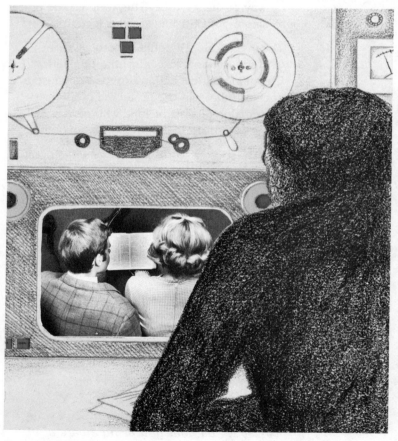

By way of electronics, Antichrist will be able to invade the privacy of your home as you have devotions! In the Tribulation Period Christians will suffer persecution and have nowhere to hide!

It is expected that very shortly *(if not already)* the technology will exist to convert your TV into a SOUND Camera. Quite possibly, in the near future, Government intelligence will be able to tap into your cable line. By pushing a series of buttons in their headquarters . . . they will be able to look right into your home by way of the TV tube! They will also be able to single out Christians for persecution!

Thus . . . cable TV could become a part of a U.S. spy network to control the population. Christian political action groups will cause a backlash that will trigger an era of intense persecution against anyone who names the name of Christ.

Antichrist . . . a world leader . . . will stop at no means to control those who pose a threat to his successes! We already have highly sophisticated spying devices. *After all, if it is now possible to make a CHIP the size of your thumbnail . . . that can make a Computer TALK . . . does it seem anymore sensational to transform your TV into a SPYING device for a Government leader?*

One Pennsylvania township as recently as October. 1980 was already considering using Cable TV networks to enable police to electronically check what they termed *"trouble-spots."* The most frightening aspect of this entire plan . . . is that this SPY PROGRAM can be carried on through your TV set . . . ***without you being aware of it!*** While you are watching a TV program . . . BIG BROTHER will be watching and listening to you!

When will Antichrist be revealed?

There have been many views expounded on exactly who Antichrist will be.

However, it is important to keep in mind that Antichrist will **not** be revealed until after the Rapture (When the saints rise to meet Christ in the air).

After the Christians are taken up from earth to meet Christ at the Rapture—then the person of Antichrist will be identified and revealed. According to 2 Thessalonians 2:4, the proof of his identity comes when he sits in the rebuilt Temple in Jerusalem and declares himself to be God.

What will be the first move of Antichrist?

One of the first moves of the Antichrist will be to gain the confidence of the Jewish people and others by his diplomatically settling the then explosive Middle East situation.

Therefore, his first attempt is to gain the favor of the Jewish people.

After accomplishing this, he will help the Jewish people immeasurably probably by returning many of them to the land of Israel and he will show them many favors.

Actually the Tribulation Period will begin with a public appearance of Antichrist when he participates in the making of a significant seven year Middle East peace pact (Daniel 9:27). At this time, however, he will not yet be recognized as the Antichrist. This recognition awaits another 3½ years (Matthew 24:15).

This individual will eventually be the head of what may be known as the Federated States of Europe. As the head of this organization, he would be able to exert great authority and power by attempting to settle the Arab-Israeli dispute.

Will Antichrist bring peace?

One thing is certain from the many references found regarding the Antichrist in the Scriptures: He will be a counterfeit and a clever imitation of the true Christ.

His rise will be sudden
This also will be an imitation of Christ.

You will recall that Christ for 30 years remained in obscurity in his home in Nazareth and the silence of those years is broken only once in Luke 2.

Comparatively, the Antichrist will also remain in obscurity and then suddenly his rise will be brought into prominence. He may even now be in the world and preparing for his Satan-directed work.

Undoubtedly one of the elements of his marvelous success in gaining the hearts of the people lies in the fact that he will come promising the very thing that is uppermost in the hearts of people all over the world today: PEACE!

This man, in the person of Antichrist, will accomplish this very thing . . . but what most people do not realize is that this accomplishment will be only for a little season—and then the very gates of hell will break loose here on earth.

Undoubtedly Antichrist will be an extremely popular individual. One only has to remember Henry Kissinger as insight. Even though Kissinger was unable to achieve peace, and returned in defeat in March, 1975, popularity polls still showed him even more popular than the President of the United States!

With Antichrist finally being able to bring peace to the Middle East; at least a semblance of peace . . . his popularity will soar!

Imagine if today some great personage would rise and almost overnight resolve the Arab-Israel crisis to the satisfaction of everyone. The Arabs would go back to developing their land, and the Israeli army could at least reduce its forces to a few thousand . . . what a triumphal victory for the negotiator!

That's what Antichrist will be able to achieve. He will be a brilliant diplomat but also a superb strategist in the art of war.

How this event may occur. These illustrations are from **666 Pictorial** by Salem Kirban. If you wish this book, send $4 to: Salem Kirban, Inc., Kent Road, Huntingdon Valley, Penna. 19006. Price includes postage and packing.

Will Antichrist be a resurrected individual?

Some have held that Antichrist will be the reincarnation of Nero. Others insist he will be Judas restored to life. The world waits.

It must be remembered that Satan does not have the power to give life. Since Christ alone has the power of resurrection, Satan could not bring one back to life unless it were by some divine permission and enablement. The wicked will not be resurrected until the Great White Throne judgment (Revelation 20:11–15). If a wicked one were resurrected in the beginning of the Tribulation Period it would set aside God's normal divinely ordained program of resurrection.

J. Dwight Pentecost in THINGS TO COME argues that *"Since all the references to this individual present him as a man, not as a supernatural being, it seems impossible to hold that he is a resurrected individual. It would be concluded that Antichrist will **not** be a resurrected individual."*

Antichrist, however, according to Revelation 13:3, 12, 14 will in some way be slain during the Tribulation Period and then he somehow will be restored back to life—imitating perhaps the resurrection of Christ! In this sense alone we could say that Anti-christ (the Beast) will be a restored-to-life being.

Who Is Antichrist?

The Bible does give us some key characteristics that will expose his true identity as Antichrist.

1. He will be popular and worshipped!
". . . the whole earth was amazed and followed after the beast (Antichrist) . . . and they worshipped the beast . . ." (Revelation 13:3, 4).

2. He will be fearless!
". . . Who is the beast (Antichrist), and who is able to wage war with him?" (Revelation 13:4).

3. He will persecute the Tribulation Saints!
"And it was given to him to make war with the saints and to overcome them . . ." (Revelation 13:7).

4. He will be a world dictator!
". . . authority over every tribe and people and tongue and nation was given to him" (Revelation 13:7).

5. He will be a maker of peace treaties!
"And he will make a firm covenant (treaty) with many for one week (one "seven year period") with Israel!" (Daniel 9:27).

6. He will not honor his peace treaty.
". . . in the middle of the week (at 3½ years) he will put a stop to sacrifice . . . and on the wing of abominations will come one who makes desolate, even until a complete destruction . . . is poured out on the one who makes desolate" (Daniel 9:27).

7. He will have no respect for the religion of his race; nor will he embrace any religious conviction!
"And he will show no regard for the gods of his fathers . . . nor will he show regard for any other god; for he will magnify himself above them all" (Daniel 11:37).

8. He will change territorial boundaries!
". . . he will give great honor to those who acknowledge him, and he will cause them to rule over many, and shall divide the land for gain" (Daniel 11:39).

9. He will be a skilled negotiator!
"And at the latter end of their kingdom, when the transgressors (the apostate Jews) have reached the fullness (of their wickedness, exceeding the limits of God's mercy), a king of fierce countenance and understanding dark trickery and craftiness, shall stand up" (Daniel 8:23).

10. His armies will be destroyed and he will be cast alive into the Lake of Fire!
"And the beast (Antichrist) was seized, and with him the false prophet who performed the signs in his presence, by which he deceived those who had received the mark of the beast (666) and those who worshipped his image; these two were thrown alive into the lake of fire which burns with brimstone. And the rest were killed with the sword . . ." (Revelation 19:20, 21).

Will Antichrist Conquer The World With A Vast Programmed Army Of Robots?

The Japanese have done it again! This time they have created machines that can actually *talk!* Computer experts have already created robots that can walk. But now the Japanese have invented one that will actually *TALK!*

For years computer scientists have been working to perfect a walking, talking robot. This computer magazine, Interface Age, devoted much of the April, 1978 issue to robots.

Robots are <u>manlike mechanical beings.</u>

Interface Age says: <u>*"Robotics are the next logical step for mankind!"*</u>

The Japanese have now invented a "talking chip." The "chip" is a very small electronic board about the size of your thumbnail. Within this small "chip" the Japanese are able to incorporate words. The amazing thing is that these "chips" are being programmed not only to talk but to talk with the proper <u>tonal</u> qualities! In this way, they will sound like a human voice and will be indistinguishable . . . that is <u>you will not be</u> <u>able to distinguish whether the talking is</u> <u>coming from a human voice or a</u> <u>computerized talking chip!</u>

You will recall that during the Tribulation Period . . . Antichrist receives a <u>*"wound to*</u> <u>*death; and his deadly wound was healed: and*</u> <u>*all the world wondered after the beast*</u> (Antichrist)" <u>Revelation 13:3,4.</u> Quite possibly Antichrist will die from this wound and the False Prophet and his associates will have devised a robot that talks and walks just as Antichrist did. Or a robot will be used until he is fully recovered.

It is also entirely possible for Antichrist to control an army made up of mechanical robots. The technology exists today . . . to produce robots that both walk and talk! They can be programmed to do the bidding of Antichrist. For their panel board will be so constructed that all orders will come from the command post at Antichrist head-quarters. Without blinking an eye this army of robots could march and overrun an army. "Casualties" would be replaced by spare parts. Thus robots would be sacrificed in an all-out advance on cities . . . without any loss of life or expensive armament. They could carry small nuclear devices that would flatten anything within 50 miles as well as blow them to bits!

Each robot will be identical and will follow identically each command! Implanted in them will be individual reaction command modules. This will enable them to INDIVIDUALLY react to certain changing conditions. Thus, they could sidestep artillery fire, dodge an oncoming enemy soldier and shoot a deadly laser ray on anything that moves in front of them! In the 6th trumpet judgment . . . during the Tribulation Period . . . a 200 MILLION Asiatic army will kill over 2 BILLION people. Will this be an army of walking, talking robots?

What or who is the "little horn" described in Daniel 7:8, 20?

Antichrist is the little horn of Daniel 7. His power will be extensive for he will gain control of the confederation of 10 nations as described in both Daniel 7 and Revelation 17:12.

This powerful leader will unite these nations . . . bringing order out of disorder . . . peace out of threatened war. For a brief time he will bring to the earth the longed-for rest and prosperity the nations desire.

The little horn (Antichrist) will make war on those living during the Tribulation Period who turn in faith to Christ (Daniel 7:24–25; Revelation 13:5–8). His associate, the False Prophet (a religious leader), will demand that everyone on earth worship Antichrist. Those who refuse will face starvation and death (Revelation 13:11–18).

Has A Mark Identification System Been Devised?

YES! There already has been developed an unusual machine which provides quick identification.

In the coming "cashless society," it will be absolutely essential that the dispensers of goods and services be able to quickly and positively identify those who offer credit cards and checks in payment. A manufacturing Company in Connecticut has developed an electronic machine that, unattended and automatically, performs verification with what is described as scientific accuracy.

Identity of the prospective purchaser or check-casher is established by the geometry of a person's hand. A person granted a

THANKS FOR SHOPPING

ROCKLEDGE PA
STORE #14   10/16/80

1/2 GAL MILK   .94F
MINESTRONI   .50F
     ia2/1.00
MINESTRONI   .50F
     ia2/1.00
NATURE SNAX   2.00F
     683/1.00
FRZ   28.47   .94F
NBC NAB CRKR   .89F
NBC NAB CRKR   .89F

     TOTAL   6.66

     CASH   7.00

     CHANGE   .34

0295 54 2 3.50PM

In October, 1980, I made the above purchases in a supermarket that had just installed a computerized cash register using a laser beam to read the vertical product markings. Without any pre-planning on my part . . . the total purchase was **666!**

The automatic scanner pictured above automatically reads the Universal Product Code. As the product is passed over the plate, a laser beam shines in all directions through the **X** opening. What the customer cannot see is the warning label that appears underneath this **X** plate. It reads: DIRECT LASAR RADIATION. Years from now we will learn it caused cancer in those we love . . . including our children!

Hand Scan
Machine
Checks
Individual
Identity

credit card, check-cashing ID card, security pass, etc., puts his right hand into the Identimat device (photo) that mechanically measures the geometry of the hand and reduces these unique measurements to an electronic code (magnetic or optical markings) which are placed in the individual's credit or ID card.

And he causeth all, both small and great, rich and poor, free and bond, to receive a mark in their right hand, or in their foreheads:
And that no man might buy or sell, save he that had the mark, or the name of the beast, or the number of his name.
(Revelation 13:16, 17)

When the card bearer goes shopping, he establishes his credit by placing both his card and right hand into the Identimat which electronically compares the two and lights up an "accept" button, signifying the person is who the card says he is. The machine will lease for about $15 a month.

One can see how such a machine could be used by Antichrist in the Tribulation Period.

Many businessmen have privately stated such a course of unifying world finance would be more than welcome!

What is meant by Daniel 7:25 which says that Antichrist will *"think to change times and laws"*

Antichrist will no doubt want to erase many memories of the past and reorganize many aspects of human existence.

The laws he will attempt to change will be those which are the fundamental, basic conditions of a divinely ordered human society.

An example would be the headship of the man over the woman.
Antichrist will probably seek to change this.

Another is the law of marriage laid down in Genesis 2:24. Marriage is for one man and one woman. Antichrist will probably also seek to change this.

Another basic principle is the seven-day week with one day for rest. Since this system is a memorial to the Creator, Antichrist will doubtless alter it—perhaps to a "more efficient"
10 day week.

As you read of these anticipated changes . . . can you not already see trends occurring in this direction?

QUESTIONS ASKED ME ON
THE TRIBULATION PERIOD

How Will People Be Saved After The Rapture?

Immediately after the Rapture of the believers (the Christians), there will not be *one single individual on earth who with true saving faith acknowledges Jesus Christ as his personal Saviour and Lord.*

Those left on earth will be those who have not trusted in God's way of salvation. This will start the Tribulation Period of 7 years. It will be one of the darkest hours for man on earth.

But God's message of salvation will be made known to them. And 7 years later . . .

So many people who have lived during the Tribulation Period will be saved (accept Christ as Lord), that the Bible says they will form

a great multitude,
which no man could number
of all nations, of
kindreds (tribes)
and tongues (languages)
　　　　　　—(Revelation 7:9-10).

Think of it! What a harvest of souls. Seven years before . . . not one person a Christian . . . but at the end of seven years those saved comprise a multitude which NO MAN COULD NUMBER!

How Does It Come About?

After the Rapture occurs, there are no believers. Therefore there are no true Christian missionaries; there are no truly born-again ministers nor evangelists.

How Will the Holy Spirit Work?

The Holy Spirit will work as in Old Testament times. And while at the Rapture (taking up of the believers) the Holy Spirit's dwelling in the believers has been removed from the earth

. . . He will still be in the world . . . just as He was in Old Testament times before Pentecost. People will be saved during the Tribulation . . . precisely as people were saved during the Old Testament times.

These first believers after the Rapture will be severely persecuted. Quite possibly they will be converted Jews (Matthew 25:40). Few will listen to them (2 Thessalonians 2:1–12) and many of them will die for their testimony and become martyrs.

Who Are the 144,000?

However, God supernaturally, places His seal on 144,000 Israelites; 12,000 from each of the 12 tribes of Israel. This is described in Revelation 7:3–8. We are told in verse 3 that this seal guarantees their safety and freedom from harm from *God's* judgments which fall in the Tribulation Period.

While Jews today may not know their tribal lineage, God does and that is what is important . . . and He will reveal it in His time.

Now keep in mind, right now, there are Jews in every part of the world. Actually in every nation and in every language we find physical descendants of Abraham. Those who are part of the 144,000 will be able to immediately witness in their area without having to go to language school. They will know the culture and language as well as the people.

Near the beginning of the Tribulation Period God will set these 144,000 apart for this special evangelistic ministry. These 144,000 will spread to the world the message of the gospel of salvation by grace through faith.

Because Antichrist will be successful in bringing a semblance of peace in this initial 3½ years of the Tribulation . . . relatively few out of the world's **billions** will pay attention to the 144,000. Quite possibly, the shock of the Rapture will be soon forgotten, and these witnesses will be ridiculed and laughed at.

How this event may occur! These illustrations are from 666 Pictorial by Salem Kirban. If you wish this book, send $4 to Salem Kirban, Inc., Kent Road, Huntingdon Valley, Pennsylvania 19006. Price includes postage and packing.

Why Are There Two Witnesses?

During the 7-year Tribulation Period God will call TWO WITNESSES (Revelation 11:3–7). These witnesses are raised up to testify mightily for God at this time. They will doubtlessly spur forward the missionary work of the 144,000.

For 3½ years these Two Witnesses will testify—perhaps from Jerusalem. They will be able to perform miracles not only to protect themselves from harm but also to destroy by fire those who oppose their ministry (Revelation 11:5–6).

When the Seal, Trumpet and Vial judgments occur during the 7 years of the Tribulation Period . . . many at this time will realize these are judgments of God . . . and will by the witness of the 144,000, accept the Lord Jesus Christ as their personal Saviour.

At the end of the 3½-year period of their ministry, Revelation 11 tells us that God will allow the Two Witnesses to be killed and their bodies will lay exposed in the streets of Jerusalem for 3½ days. At the end of the 3½ days, they will rise and ascend to Heaven to the amazement of everyone. Read Revelation 11:11.

THE JUDGMENTS OF THE TRIBULATION PERIOD

	First Seal	Second Seal	Third Seal	Fourth Seal	Fifth Seal	Sixth Seal	Seventh Seal
First 3½ Years — After The Rapture comes... **The Seven Seal Judgments**	Rider on White Horse Peace—Antichrist	Rider on Red Horse War	Rider on Black Horse Famine	Rider on Pale Horse Death	Martyred Souls Persecution	Changes on Earth Destruction	Silence ∙∙∙ 7 Trumpets Appear

	First Trumpet	Second Trumpet	Third Trumpet	Fourth Trumpet	Fifth Trumpet	Sixth Trumpet	Seventh Trumpet
From out of the Seventh Seal comes... **The Seven Trumpet Judgments**	⅓ Earth afire ⅓ Trees burned All grass burned	Meteor destroys ⅓ ships, fish—⅓ sea—blood filled	Falling Star poisons ⅓ of all water	⅓ of sun, moon and stars darkened	5 months of torture by Scorpion stings	Satan's 200 million army kills ⅓ Mankind	Earthquake 7000 die in Jerusalem

	First Vial	Second Vial	Third Vial	Fourth Vial	Fifth Vial	Sixth Vial	Seventh Vial
Last 3½ Years — From out of the Seventh Trumpet comes... **The Seven Vial Judgments**	Boils affect those with Mark of Antichrist	Sea of Blood Everything in ocean dies	Rivers of Blood Rivers, springs turn to blood	Heat from Sun scorches all Mankind	Darkness Earth plunged into darkness	River Euphrates Dried up—Army attacks Israel	Hail Cities crumble

How does the United States fit into Bible prophecy?

There are those who believe that certain references in prophecy to far-off places point to the United States. Others identify the harlot of Revelation 17 with apostate Christendom and then stretch the point implying that the "mother of harlots" is the United States.

However there is no specific prophecy regarding the United States in future events. It is quite possible that with the rising threat of Russia, the United States will find it necessary to merge with the European Common Market countries and become one of the 10 nations in the United States of Europe which will follow the Antichrist in his "Beast" confederation of nations (Revelation 13:1; 17:12).

The idea which some have advocated, that the United States is the so-called Israeli "lost" tribe of Manasseh is totally void of intelligent or historically bonafide proof. Orthodox Bible scholars, historians, and Jews alike reject it as a fabulous fabrication. (See **Doctrines of Devils, Number 1, Armstrong's Church of God** (The Plain Truth)/an expose by Salem Kirban. Armstrong is one advocate of this false theory that the United States is Manasseh.)*

---

*For a copy of **Armstrong's Church of God** (The Plain Truth) by Salem Kirban send $4 to: Salem Kirban. Inc. Kent Road, Huntingdon Valley, Pennsylvania 19006. includes postage.

Identify the 3 personages in Revelation 12. What is the identity of the "Woman?"

1. A great red dragon (Revelation 12:3-4, 9) Look at verse 9. This makes the identification of this individual certain. The great red dragon is Satan. In verse 7 we see that Satan is at war with the heavenly host, seeking a governmental authority over the woman's *"remnant,"* which authority rightly belongs to Christ Himself.

2. A man child (Revelation 12:5-6; Psalm 2) The child here in Revelation 12:5 is to rule all nations with a rod of iron. In Psalm 2—a Messianic Psalm—verse 9 shows that the one to rule the nations with the rod of iron is Christ. Thus it identifies the man child of Revelation 12 as none other than Jesus Christ.

3. A woman clothed with the sun (Revelation 12:13-17) There have been many false conjectures as to the identity of this woman. Some believed it was Mary (yet she was never protected for 1260 days, nor did she ever flee into the wilderness). Others have held that this is the Church travailing to bring Christ to the nations. This has no foundation and must be rejected. The Church did not produce Christ, but Christ the church.

We believe that the woman in this passage represents the nation Israel. The use of the term *woman* frequently appears in the Old Testament referring to the nation Israel. See Isaiah 47:7-9; 54:5-6; 66:7-8; Jeremiah 4:31; Micah 4:9-10; 5:3. While

the church is called a *bride,* we never find
the church referred to as a *woman.*

The decisive evidence proving that Israel is
the woman, however, is found in Genesis
37:9–10. Here and here alone in the Bible
do we see the source for the sun, moon,
and 12-star motif which this woman of
Revelation wears. In Genesis 37 the same
symbols represent the nation Israel—as
they must here also. **The woman is the
nation Israel** which during the Tribulation
will be persecuted by Satan and then
rescued by God as she turns again to her
Messiah (Zechariah 12:10).

What is the Satanic trinity?

Just as there is a Heavenly Trinity (Father,
Son and Holy Spirit), the Bible reveals that
there is also a Satanic trinity (Satan, the
Antichrist, and the False Prophet).

1. **Satan** imitates the work of **God the
   Father.**
2. **The Beast (Antichrist)** imitates the work of
   the **Son** in dying, being resurrected, and in
   subjecting the world to himself. The Bible
   sometimes refers to Antichrist as The
   Beast because he becomes the leader of
   the end-time Beast empire (Daniel 7;
   Revelation 13). He will be a human being
   inspired by Satan.
3. **The False Prophet** imitates the work of
   the **Holy Spirit** in glorifying the Son
   (Antichrist) and in sealing those who trust
   in him.

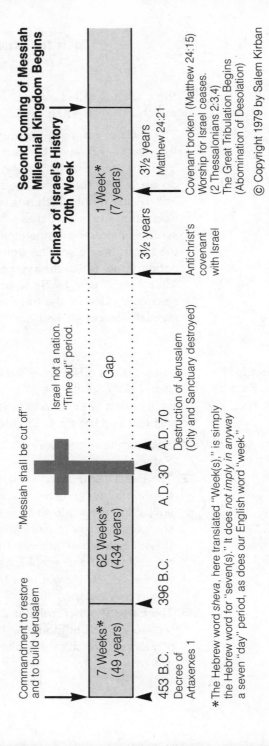

Seventieth Week of Daniel

Commandment to restore and to build Jerusalem

"Messiah shall be cut off"

Israel not a nation. "Time out" period.

Second Coming of Messiah
Millennial Kingdom Begins

Climax of Israel's History
70th Week

| 7 Weeks* (49 years) | 62 Weeks* (434 years) | Gap | 3½ years | 1 Week* (7 years) | 3½ years |

453 B.C.
Decree of
Artaxerxes 1

396 B.C.

A.D. 30

A.D. 70
Destruction of Jerusalem
(City and Sanctuary destroyed)

Antichrist's covenant with Israel

Covenant broken. (Matthew 24:15)
Worship for Israel ceases.
(2 Thessalonians 2:3,4)
The Great Tribulation Begins
(Abomination of Desolation)

Matthew 24:21

© Copyright 1979 by Salem Kirban

*The Hebrew word *sheva*, here translated "Week(s)," is simply the Hebrew word for "seven(s)." It does *not imply in anyway* a seven "day" period, as does our English word "week."

WHAT IS MEANT BY
THE 70 WEEKS OF DANIEL?

The 9th chapter of Daniel relates the 70 weeks of prophecy. The prophecy of the 70 weeks refers to 70 sevens of years, or 490 years. In Hebrew the word *Shavoah* means *"seven"* of anything—it is simply the number 7—or it can mean a *"week,"* Thus Daniel 9:24 more literally reads *"Seventy sevens"* rather than *"Seventy weeks."*

The 70 weeks was to be divided into three parts:

1. 49 years (7x7) **7 WEEKS** Starting Point of This Prophecy. The first period of 49 years would begin with *"the commandment to restore and to build Jerusalem."* This commandment was very possibly some decree issued in 453 B.C., before the one by Artaxerxes in 445 B.C. At that time Artaxerxes gave Nehemiah permission to build *"the wall of the city"* (Nehemiah 2:8, 13-5). From the time of this decree to the close of the Old Testament canon (Malachi) . . . covers 49 years or 7x7.

2. 434 years (62x7) **62 WEEKS**
Combining the first cycle of 49 years with the second cycle of 434 years . . . we have a total of 483 years after the decree of Artaxerxes. We are told in Daniel 9:26 that *". . . after the [additional] threescore and two weeks (483 years) shall Messiah be cut off."* This period clearly ends at 30 A.D. with the "cutting off," crucifixion and atoning death, of Christ.

Thus far we have observed 69 weeks of Daniel.

3. 7 years **1 WEEK**
The 69 weeks in Section 1 and 2 seem to have run their course successively, without interruption.

The 70th weeks does not begin until Antichrist makes his peace pact—*"the covenant"*—with Israel (Daniel 9:27). *"In the midst of the week"* the Antichrist shall break the treaty and commit what is called the Abomination of Desolation in the rebuilt Temple (Matthew 24:15; 2 Thessalonians 2:3-4).

Between the 69th week of Daniel and the 70th week of Daniel there is an interval of time. It runs from Christ's death to the events opening this final Seventieth Week of Daniel. We are presently living during this time interval . . . right now. This will end at the Rapture.

Will the Tribulation take place _immediately_ after the Rapture?

In the prophetic calendar the Tribulation is the next event after the Rapture of the church. Looking at Daniel 9 we see a break in the continuity of the 70 week of years prophecy. This break comes between week 69 and 70.

The 69th* week of years ends with the death of Christ (_"Messiah . . . cut off"_) and thus is long past. The events of the 70th week of 7 years with Antichrist making a treaty involving Israel and then breaking it after 3½ years have not yet occurred.

Thus, since the event closing the 69th week is long past and the event marking the start of the 70th week has not yet taken place, there is a gap between the 69th week of Bible prophecy and the 70th week (which is the Tribulation Period). We are living in this _"gap"_ era.

This _"parenthesis"_ or _"gap"_ will end at the time of the Rapture. Then, at any time after that the Tribulation Period of 7 years can begin. Daniel 9:24–27 and Revelation 8:8, 10 seem to indicate that the Tribulation Period will begin immediately after the Rapture.

*(For those who wish to study the complex Daniel 9 passage—Daniel 9:26 speaks of the 62 weeks which follow the initial 7 weeks described in Daniel 9:25. Hence when Daniel says Messiah will be cut off after the 62 weeks, adding the previous 7, we find that it is after the 69th week when Christ was to die.)

Who Will Be Saved During the Tribulation Period?

Three groups of believers will be saved during the Tribulation. They are as follows:

1. **Early Martyrs**
   Those who are saved and martyred **during the first half of the Tribulation (Revelation 6:9–11).**

2. **144,000 From Israel**
   These 144,000 Jews are saved by God's supernatural intervention. They are sealed, protected from all harm from God's judgments, and they appear to enter into the Millennium *physically preserved* (Revelation 7 and 14).

3. **Great Multitude from All Nations**
   These are the "great multitude, which no man could number" who are saved much because of the witnessing of the 144,000. They are *martyred* during the Tribulation Period (Revelation 7:9–14).

The 144,000 servants of God are sealed in their foreheads. Antichrist, the great imitator, will also cause his followers to receive **"a mark in their right hand, or in their foreheads"** (Revelation 13:16).

Israel's Past, Present and Future

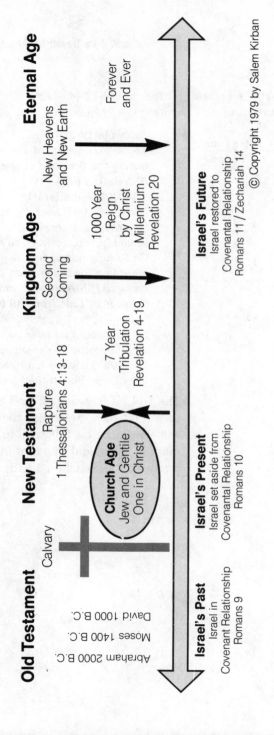

Old Testament

Calvary

Church Age
Jew and Gentile
One in Christ

Abraham 2000 B.C.
Moses 1400 B.C.
David 1000 B.C.

Israel's Past
Israel in
Covenantal Relationship
Romans 9

New Testament

Rapture
1 Thessalonians 4:13-18

7 Year
Tribulation
Revelation 4-19

Israel's Present
Israel set aside from
Covenantal Relationship
Romans 10

Kingdom Age

Second
Coming

1000 Year
Reign
by Christ
Millennium
Revelation 20

Israel's Future
Israel restored to
Covenantal Relationship
Romans 11 / Zechariah 14

Eternal Age

New Heavens
and New Earth

Forever
and Ever

© Copyright 1979 by Salem Kirban

Why is Israel a blinded nation and when will this spiritual blindness be removed?

Israel is spiritually blind because she willfully rejected Christ as her Messiah. Romans 9 through 11 is the longest New Testament discourse on this. In this case the word *blindness* implies that Israel has become callous or hardened so that the message of salvation is impenetrable as far as the nation in general is concerned.

This does not mean that individual Jews may not receive salvation, but rather that the nation as a whole has been judicially blinded.

Romans 11:25 tells us this blindness in part happened to Israel *". . . until the fullness of the Gentiles be come in."*

This means that the blindness of the nation of Israel will be taken away at some point. The Rapture of the church would seem to be that point.

When does the Battle of Gog and Magog occur?

Ezekiel 38:1–39:16 describes the Battle of Gog and Magog . . . *"Son of man, set thy face against Gog, the land of Magog."* Using the ancient names for the region which is now southwestern Russia, this passage tells of a yet future invasion by the people of this land into Palestine. Ezekiel 38:16 tells us that it will be in the latter days and 38:14 informs us that it will be a time when Israel dwells in the land safely. In 38:15 and 39:2 it is emphasized that the invaders will come from the north. This fits perfectly with Moscow being almost perfectly due north of Jerusalem. God will at that future day destroy the invading armies with fire from heaven.

The 200 million army of the East plans to attack the army of Antichrist at Armageddon. Suddenly the heavens open! The Lord comes down with His army, clothed in fine linen (Revelation 19:11-16). Antichrist's army and the Asiatic army realize they have a common enemy as they point their cannon artillery to the skies. But judgment is swift. Antichrist and the False Prophet are cast alive into the Lake of Fire. The entire army will be slain! See Revelation 19:19-21.

What a holocaust! Remember, the armies from Asia number 200 million (Revelation 9:16). Antichrist's army will also most likely have at least 200 million. Thus . . . the possible casualty rate of those slain at Armageddon could be 400 MILLION!

QUESTIONS ASKED ME ON
THE BATTLE OF ARMAGEDDON

What is the Final Alignment of Nations?

At the end of Gentile world power, during the Tribulation Period, there will be **three** kingdoms and federations of nations who contest the authority of the 10 Federated States of Europe.

1. **The Northern confederacy**
   [Ezekiel 38:1-39:25 (esp. 38:15, 39:2) Daniel 11:40; Joel 2:1-27 (esp. 2:20); Isaiah 10:12; 30:31-33; 31:8-9]

   You will find the principal passage describing this northern confederacy in Ezekiel 38:2-6.

   Basically, here are the nations in the **northern** confederacy of Ezekiel 38:
   A. Gog, Meshech, and Tubal (vs. 2) -Russia.
   B. Persia (vs. 5) - Iran and Iraq.
   C. Ethiopia and Libya (vs. 5) - Northeast Africa.
   D. Gomer (vs. 6) - Germany (possibly East Germany).
   E. Togarmah (vs. 6) - Exact location uncertain, but in the Europe, Turkey, Syria cresent.

2. **The Asiatic confederacy**
   In Revelation 16:12 we read that Palestine, which will have become the center of the activity of Antichrist and his European federation . . . will be invaded by a great army coming from beyond the Euphrates known as the forces of *"the kings of the east."*

   This is the second great alliance of powers that threatens the authority of the Federated States of Europe and Antichrist.

The nations will most likely include: China, Japan, North Korea, Vietnam, Thailand, Cambodia, and other Asian countries.

3. **The Arab confederacy**

   In Daniel 11:40 we find a third power in conflict with the European Federation of States. This is known as the King of the South. This power advances on Palestine and sets off a movement of nations that brings about its destruction. It would appear that the King of the South is Egypt aligned with other Arab nations and together allied with Russia (King of the North).

The above three alliances will challenge the ever growing power of Antichrist. Antichrist will be head of the 10 nation **United States of Europe.** This federation of states will probably include France, England, possibly West Germany and other Common Market countries. Perhaps even the United States will join this coalition of nations.

The prophecy is revealed in Revelation 17:12–13, which shows that these nations that were once a part of the Roman Empire will gather together and are going to enter into an agreement to give their authority to one man as their head (Daniel 7:7–8, 23–26 Cp. Revelation 13). **That one man will be Antichrist!**

Armageddon

Armageddon—a strange sounding name—will be the battle ground for the greatest blood bath that the world has ever seen. Armageddon (Hebrew for: "Mount Megiddo") represents a strategic valley in Northern Israel named for the nearby ancient city of Megiddo. This city built upon a hill, Mt. Megiddo, commands the Jezreel Valley and the Plain of Esdraelon. This is the gateway through the mountains from the North to Jerusalem.

When will the Battle of Armageddon occur?

It will occur at the **end** of the 7-year Tribulation Period.

How will events bring about this Battle?

During the Tribulation Period the war machine of Russian Communism will be destroyed (Ezekiel 38:1-39:16). Two world leaders will emerge. The 10-nation European Federation will elect a powerful, personable man to lead them. He will be able to bring peace in the Middle East. He will be the **Antichrist.** A religious leader will direct all worship only to the Antichrist. He will be the **False Prophet.**

Antichrist will persecute Israel, and his power will become worldwide. China and her allies, called the "Kings of the East" in Revelation 16:12, will bring an army of 200 million towards Israel with the intent of destroying Jerusalem and taking over world leadership. Antichrist, for some diabolical cause, also causes armies from all over the earth to invade Israel. Perhaps Antichrist seeks to fight the Asian alliance.

Suddenly, against both the armies of Antichrist and the armies of the East, something unusual happens. The Heavens open, Jesus Christ appears on a white horse with the armies of heaven, and destroys all these armies gathered in central Israel. More than 200 million die! The blood bath covers 185 miles of Israel! Antichrist and the False Prophet are cast into the Lake of Fire.

Thus in the Tribulation Period we will find 4 great kingdoms as follows:

1. Russia and her allies (The Northern confederacy)
2. China and her allies (The Asiatic confederacy)
3. Egypt and her allies (The Arab confederacy)
4. United States of Europe (The 10 nation confederacy).

Is the Gog and Magog Battle of Revelation 20:7-9 the same as the Gog and Magog battle described in Ezekiel 38:1-39:16?

No. The battle described in Ezekiel is an invasion that comes solely from the **North,** from Russia and her adjacent allies. At the end of this battle one-sixth of the invaders survive alive to return home (Ezekiel 39:2).

In the battle described in Revelation, however, the invaders are assembled not from the north, but from all of *"the four quarters of the earth."*
Here one-sixth of the invaders do not survive, but all are pictured as entirely annihilated by God's fury (Revelation 20:7–9).

The Ezekiel one occuring *before* the Millennial 1000 years and the one described in Revelation clearly taking place *after* the Millennial 1000 years (*"And when the 1000 years are expired . . ."*
—Revelation 20:7).

The latter invaders are called Gog and Magog in the same way that evil doers are continually referred to as *"Sons of Belial."* In the same way we use the word *"Vandal"* today for all who destroy in a wanton fashion—even though they may not be in any way related to the original tribe of Vandals who sacked North Africa in the Fifth Century A.D. Thus the Scriptures in Revelation call the wicked invaders Gog and Magog because this group will imitate the Gog and Magog invaders of 1000 years before.

Does the Bible mention a time when all men will be saved or reconciled to God?

No!

In fact the Bible makes it very plain that all men will not be saved! It speaks of the lost in the Lake of Fire enduring endless grief (Revelation 20:12-15).

Salvation can only come through acceptance of Jesus Christ as personal Lord and Saviour.

> *Neither is there salvation in any other; for there is no other name under heaven given among men, whereby we must be saved* (Acts 4:14).

While the lost in hell will be forced to bow in submission to Christ, they will not be reconciled (restored to fellowship with Christ). Instead there will be *"weeping, and wailing, and gnashing of teeth."* See Matthew 13:42,50.

What is meant by the words "this generation shall not pass till all these things be fulfilled"?

This verse is found in Matthew 24:34 and it appears to refer to the generation that shall be living immediately prior to the Rapture.

In plain language Christ is declaring that the coming period of trouble (the Tribulation Period) will not run for years and years spanning generations. No, it will rather be accomplished during the life span of one generation—the *"this generation"* of whom Christ speaks.

The idea that "this generation" refers to those then alive with Christ and the apostles must be rejected. This is so because the events described in Matthew 24:29–31 did not occur in the Apostolic Age nor, in fact, have they yet occurred. The events are still future, and hence, "this generation" is still future.

We cannot, however, set a date for the Lord's Coming (often termed Christ's Second Coming). See Mark 13:32.

We are here told that the generation which sees the beginning of the period of troubles which Christ describes in Matthew 24 will be the generation to see all these things accomplished.

This present generation now living could be that generation. Even now we may be seeing the buds which will eventually open up into the troubles of the Tribulation Period—false christs, wars, famines, mass deaths, earthquakes, and hatred toward God and all who would confess Him.

In light of this, what are you doing now to tell others of Christ's message of saving grace?

Antichrist will deceive millions during the Tribulation Period. God will send them a strong delusion that they will believe the lie (2 Thessalonians 2:11). Their complete destruction will come at the Battle of Armageddon!

Sequence of Coming Judgments

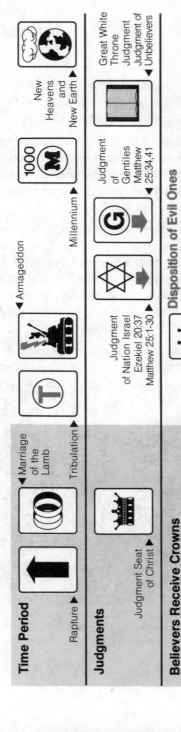

Time Period

Rapture ▲   ▼ Marriage of the Lamb   Tribulation ▲   ▼ Armageddon   Millennium ▲

New Heavens and New Earth ▲

1000 (M)

Judgments

Judgment Seat of Christ ▲

Judgment of Nation Israel Ezekiel 20:37 Matthew 25:1-30 ▲

Judgment of Gentiles Matthew 25:34,41 ▲

Great White Throne Judgment Judgment of Unbelievers ▲

Believers Receive Crowns

Crown of Rejoicing   Crown of Righteousness
(1 Thessalonians 2:19,20)   (1 Timothy 4:8)   Crown of Life
Incorruptible Crown   Crown of Glory   (Revelation 2:10)
(1 Corinthians 9:25)   (1 Peter 5:2,4)

Disposition of Evil Ones

Antichrist (the Beast) and the False Prophet (Religious Leader) cast alive into the Lake of Fire at end of the Battle of Armageddon (Revelation 19:20). Satan (the Devil) cast into the Lake of Fire at end of Millennium (Revelation 20:10).

QUESTIONS ASKED ME ON
THE JUDGMENTS

JUDGMENT DAYS

RAPTURE — BELIEVERS meet CHRIST in the air

REWARD JUDGMENTS FOR BELIEVERS

INCORRUPTIBLE CROWN (Victor's Crown)
"... every man that striveth for the mastery is temperate in all things ... they do it to obtain a corruptible crown; we an INCORRUPTIBLE." (1 Corinthians 9:25)

CROWN OF REJOICING (Soul Winner's Crown)
"... what is our hope ... or crown of rejoicing? Are not even ye in the presence of our Lord Jesus Christ at His coming? For ye are our glory and joy." (1 Thessalonians 2:19, 20)

CROWN OF RIGHTEOUSNESS
"Henceforth there is laid up for me a crown of righteousness, which the Lord, the righteous judge, shall give me at that day: and not to me only, but unto all them also that love His appearing." (II Timothy 4:8)

CROWN OF GLORY (Crown for Service)
"Feed the flock of God which is among you ... (be) examples to the flock ... And when the chief Shepherd shall appear, ye shall receive a crown of glory that fadeth not away." (1 Peter 5:2-4)

CROWN OF LIFE (Martyr's Crown)
"... the devil shall cast some of you into prison, that ye may be tried be thou faithful unto death, and I will give thee a crown of life." (Revelation 2:10)

"Every man's work shall be made manifest ... because it shall be revealed by fire ... if any man's work abide ... he shall receive a reward ... if any man's work shall be burned, he shall suffer loss: but he himself shall be saved; yet so as by fire." (1 Corinthians 3:13-15)

WOOD — HAY — STUBBLE

| SILVER | GOLD |
| PRECIOUS STONES | |

"and I will dwell in the house of the Lord forever." (Psalm 23:6)

1000 YEAR MILLENNIUM

JUDGMENT OF UNBELIEVERS

BOOK OF LIFE

THE BOOKS OPENED

"And whosoever was not found written in the book of life was cast into the Lake of Fire." (Rev. 20:15)

"... the tares are the children of the wicked one; The enemy that sowed them is the devil; the harvest is the end of the world; and the reapers are the angels. As therefore the tares are gathered and burned in the fire; so shall it be in the end of this world." (Matthew 13:38-40)

LAKE OF FIRE

JUDGMENTS and their DISTINCTION

1. Judgment of the Church *The Judgment Seat of Christ*
(2 Corinthians 5:10-11)
Here we have the judgment of the believer's works . . . not his sins.
Hebrews 10:17 tells us that the Christian's sins and iniquities will be
remembered no more. But Matthew 12:36, Romans 14:10, Colossians
3:24-25 remind us that every work must come to judgment. This
judgment **occurs at the return of Christ for His church** (Rapture)
. . . immediately after the Rapture but before the marriage supper of
the Lamb.

2. Judgment of individual Gentiles
(Matthew 25:32)
This event is fully anticipated in the Old Testament. See Psalm
2:1-10, Isaiah 63:1-6, Joel 3:2-16; Zephaniah 3:8 and Zechariah
14:1-3.

Here the sheep (believers) are separated from the goats (unbelievers). This **occurs after the Tribulation Period** when those Gentiles
who have come to Christ during this perilous period will be ushered
into the kingdom and eternal life. The goats (unbelievers) will be cast
into everlasting fire for their sins.

3. Judgment of Israel
(Ezekiel 20:33-38)
When Christ returns **after the Tribulation Period** He will regather
the Jews and purge those who rebelled. This will be accomplished
after He first delivers the whole nation from its persecutors. Those
who, like the sheep among the Gentiles, are believers in Jesus Christ
will be ushered into the kingdom.

4. Judgment of the Wicked *The Great White Throne Judgment*
(Revelation 20:11-15)
For this judgment we look to the time **after the Millennium** (1000
years). This last judgment comes to all unbelievers of all ages at the
Great White Throne. The Holy God, the Sovereign Judge, will be
seated on the throne. These unbelievers will be judged according to
their sinful works. And because not one of them has his name written
in the Lamb's book of life . . . they will be cast into the lake of fire.

There will be no escape forever!

(Top left) Petra is surrounded by the rugged mountains of Edom. The valley is entered by the Siq—a narrow defile in the red sandstone cliffs. At some places this narrow entrance is only 8 feet wide. Photo at right reveals high red sandstone cliffs which rise 200 to 300 feet. *(Bottom left)* Diane Kirban on horseback. Note numerous caves in background. The area is virtually impregnable from any land attack. See Mark 13:14.

**Will the
Temple
be rebuilt?**

In A.D. 70 the Romans destroyed Jerusalem and the Temple. Since that time Jews have beseeched God four times in a week in their synagogues to *"Renew our days as they once were."* In essence this is a plea for the restoration of the Temple.

Israel has had no Temple since 70 A.D.

One of the main obstructions to the rebuilding of the Temple is that the Temple must be built on its original site. And on its original site is now the Dome of the Rock . . . the familiar gold domed building that dominates the Jerusalem skyline. This is Islam's sacred spot. The Mohammedans believe the rock formation inside the Dome of the Rock is the place from which Mohammed ascended to heaven.

Perhaps through an earthquake or some similar disaster which may demolish this Dome of the Rock Israel will again have access to this location. Then during the first half of the Tribulation Period, if not before, they will be able to once again build the Temple.

But in the middle of the Tribulation Period Antichrist will desecrate the Temple . . . perhaps by placing his own image in it and causing the people to worship him and bear his mark of allegiance (Daniel 9:27; Matthew 24:15; 2 Thessalonians 2:3–4).

It is at this time (Matthew 24:16) when many Jews will *". . . flee into the mountains."* Some have suggested that these mountains refer to Petra which is presently in Jordan and just about 50 miles south of Jerusalem.

What happens to those unbelievers who have already died,
who will die today, tomorrow or anytime in the future before
their Final Judgment after the 1000 year Millennium?

Dr. J. Dwight Pentecost in his book THINGS TO COME points
out that there are four different words used in Scriptures to
describe the place of the dead until their resurrection at the
Great White Throne Judgment at the close of the Millennium;
Sheol, Hades, Tartaros, and Gehenna.

These four words do NOT always refer to the eternal state of
"the Lake of Fire" (which begins after the 1000 year Millennium) but rather often to the temporary place in which the
dead await their resurrection. Here are those words:

1. SHEOL
   This is used 65 times in the Old Testament of which 31
   times it is translated "grave."

2. HADES (literally, the "unseen" world.)
   This is used generally to describe the unsaved dead who are
   awaiting the resurrection unto the Great White Throne. In
   every instance but one it is translated as "hell."

3. TARTAROS
   This word is only used once in Scripture (2 Peter 2:4) and
   refers to the place wherein the wicked angels are held in
   prison awaiting their final judgment.

4. GEHENNA
   This is used 12 times in the New Testament. (Matthew 5:22,
   29-30, Mark 9:43, etc.) It is a representation of the final
   place of judgment for the Lost.

[In the Hebrew this word literally means "Valley" (Ge) "of Hen-
non" (Henna). Its fires burning the garbage of Jerusalem provided Christ with the perfect picture of the eternal doom of
those who are lost.]

The unbelieving dead are right now in torment and in misery
in their temporary place of punishment—Hades or Hell (Luke
16:19-31). Here they await their final resurrection after the
1000 year Millennial reign of Christ which will then be immediately followed by the Great White Throne judgment and
their eternal condemnation to the Lake of Fire (Revelation
20:11-15).

Is There a Millennium Temple?

Ezekiel 40:1–46:24 describes another Temple which will be built during the Millennium. Many details are given in these chapters on its structure, its priesthood, it ritual and its ministry.

This temple will also be located in the city of Jerusalem, on Mount Moriah. This shall be the *"mountain of Jehovah's house,"* established on the *"top of the mountain"* and *"exalted above the hills,"* into which all nations shall flow (Isaiah 2:4; Ezekiel 37:26; Micah 4:1–4).

Ezekiel 40 to 42 tells us that the entire area will be enclosed by a wall. There will be three outer gates, north, south and east, each of which is entered by 7 steps. There shall be no gate on the west side—the side of the present Wailing Wall (Ezekiel 40:24).

Dr. Merrill F. Unger suggests there are 5 purposes of the Millennial Temple:

1. To Demonstrate God's Holiness
2. To Provide a Dwelling Place for the Divine Glory (Ezekiel 43:7)
3. To Perpetuate the Memorial of Sacrifice
4. To Provide the Center for the Divine Government
5. To Provide Victory over the Curse (Ezekiel 47:1–12)

This Temple is the Temple erected in the Millennium.

Is There a Temple _After_ the Millennium?

After the Millennium, with the New Heavens and New Earth, there will be **no** Temple. Revelation 21:22).

In 2 Chronicles 7 we read of the dedication of the Temple which Solomon built (10th century B.C.). From it, as well as from other places in the Scripture, we can see that the Temple was a place wherein the holy God would dwell in a special way in the midst of His people. Because all the inhabitants of the earth were sinners God's holiness demanded some type of isolation from this sin—this the Temple provided. But since God was a merciful God who was willing to forgive His people for their sins when they called upon His name in repentance and prayer, the Temple also provided a localized manifestation of His presence where this could be done.

In the world to come, however, since all sinners will have already been excluded at the Great White Throne judgment and since the New Earth will never have been touched by sin's defilement, there will no more be a need for a Temple building. There will no more be a need for God to be isolated from His people—for they will all be sinless. Thus the ever omnipresent God will fill the New Jerusalem, and in fact the entire New Earth, with His manifest presence. Now the cubical New Jerusalem with all of its hugeness becomes the inner Holy of Holies where the Lord abides, and the entire New Earth becomes the outer Holy Place wherein the Lord also dwells _(Revelation Visualized_ on Revelation 21:22).

The Millennium will not yet be heaven. Compare Isaiah 65:20 with Revelation 21:4 to see this. The government of the Millennium will be a *theocracy*.

A *theocracy* is a government in which God is recognized as the supreme civil ruler and His laws are taken as the laws of the state. And the Lord will choose Jerusalem to be the center of all spiritual blessing (Zechariah 2:12; 8:22; 14:16).

In the Millennium will be **3** classes of people:

1. All the **saved** of **Israel alive**
   at the end of the 7-year Tribulation Period.

2. All the **saved** of the **Gentiles alive**
   at the end of the 7-year Tribulation Period.

These people in listing **1** and **2** will have **natural bodies.**

3. **The Believers who have died before the Rapture.**
   These resurrected saints will have positions of responsibility in the Millennium (Matthew 19:28; Luke 19:27-27). They will have **resurrected bodies.**

Living believers (Listing 1 and 2) will be able to marry and be given in marriage. The women will reproduce and have children. These children born in the Millennium will be given an opportunity to accept Christ or reject Him at the end of the Millennium. A vast number will reject Him and follow Satan (Revelation 20:7, 8).

Life in the Millennium will be one of **peace** (Isaiah 11:6-9), **happiness** (Isaiah 11:6-9; Revelation 20:3) and **long life and health** (Isaiah 33:24; 35:5, 6; 65:20; Jeremiah 30:19, 20).

The New Heavens and New Earth follows the Millennium.

Where will resurrected Believers live during the Millennium?

Some excellent Bible teachers believe they will reign in Heaven. However, Matthew 19:28 seems to indicate that we who are caught up in the Rapture will actually reign on earth with Christ during the 1000 years.

Will children born of *Living Believers* during the Millennium be tempted by Satan when he is loosed at the end of the Millennium period

Yes. There will be children born to those living believers who enter the kingdom and these children will be born with the Adamic, sinful nature (Isaiah 65:20). They, even in the near perfect environment of that day, still need to believe and be saved.

Also you must remember that the Millennium is 1000 years long. Those born even as late as 18 years prior to the end of the 1000 years Millennium will not be little children, but actually adults, at the time of this final Satanic temptation. During this 1000 years Satan will be in the bottomless pit. But then God will release him.

After living in 1000 years of prosperity, wealth, health and very little death . . . an abundance of everything . . . **Some still will not believe and are still not satisfied.** And Satan will deceive them into believing he can offer them something better. And so clever is his deception that he musters an army **As Numerous as the Sands of the Sea!** These will be children of the *Living Believers* (Revelation 20:7–10).

THREE VIEWS ON THE MILLENNIUM

THE MILLENNIUM POSITIONS	WHAT DOES IT MEAN	WHAT EACH GROUP BELIEVES	OBJECTION OR SUPPORT
POST MILLENNIALISM	Christ will come to establish His Kingdom on Earth AFTER (Post) the 1000 Years (Millennium).	The earth will get better and better through the spread of the Gospel, and Christ will come to claim His Kingdom after 1000 years of peace has transpired.	Naïve. The earth is not getting better; and the Bible does not teach that it is (II Timothy 3:1-7).
A MILLENNIALISM	There will be NO FUTURE Earthly 1000 year Reign (Millennium). (In Greek "A" at the beginning of a word means "NO.")	The Millennium is *NOW!* Peace on earth exists in the Church; and Satan is NOW bound so that he cannot prevent the spread of the Gospel.	Revelation 20:3 says that Satan goes to prison "that he should deceive the nations no more." Look at Cuba, China and Russia. Satan is not NOW in prison.
PRE MILLENNIALISM	Christ will come personally to judge the wicked and to establish His Kingdom BEFORE (Pre) the 1000 years (Millennium) begins.	The earth is getting worse, and the Kingdom age cannot begin until Christ comes to destroy the wicked.	This is the teaching of the Bible. Christ will come (Revelation 19: 11-21) and then the Kingdom will be set up (Revelation 20).

THESE POSITIONS HAVE *NOTHING* TO DO WITH THE SALVATION OF A SINNER.

Isaiah 65:20 speaks of a child dying at 100 years of age and a sinner being accursed at that age. What does this mean?

The first part of the verse seems to indicate that during the Millennium no one shall die in infancy. The span of life will be greatly increased. Revelation 22:2 indicates that in the final eternal state healing will be available for any illness. This doubtless also will be true to a great extent in the Millennium.

One who dies at the age of 100 will be considered to have died as a child. *"The sinnerbeing a hundred years old shall be accursed"*—would indicate that death at a 100 years in the Millennium will be looked upon as a youthful premature tragedy.

During this age death seems never to be by natural causes alone but will be the result of the judgment of God. Psalm 101:8 tells *"I will early destroy all the wicked of the land, that I may cut off all wicked doers from the city of the LORD."*

Some have suggested that this means that every morning there will be summary judgment of all wickedness. They advance that one who commits a transgression will have until the following morning to repent and make the matter right. This, however, seems to be reading details into this verse far beyond which it plainly teaches.

However, we must wait until the Millennium, or at least until the Rapture, for complete clarity on such questions.

THE RESURRECTIONS

Heaven

Resurrection and Ascension of Christ into Heaven
(Matthew 27:52-53 tells of others who were resurrected after Christ—these were the wave-sheaf of the harvest to come. Leviticus 23:10-11).
Acts 1:1-11
Matthew 27:50-53

Paradise

Believers who have died before the Rapture. Present in a celestial, spiritual body.*

"And Jesus said unto him, Verily I say unto thee, Today shalt thou be with me in paradise."
Luke 23:43

"We are confident, I say, and willing rather to be absent from the body, and to be present with the Lord."
2 Corinthians 5:8

Believers meet with Christ in the air
1 Thessalonians 4:16

"...the dead in Christ shall rise First:"
"Then we which are alive and remain shall be caught up together with them in the clouds to meet the Lord in the air:..." 1 Thessalonians 4:16-17

Judgment Seat of Christ

"For we must all appear before the judgment seat of Christ:..."
2 Corinthians 5:10
Believers now in New Bodies
Philippians 3:20-21

Resurrection of Tribulation Saints
Daniel 12:1-2

Marriage of the Lamb
Revelation 19:7-9

Christ Returns to Earth with His Saints
1 Thessalonians 3:13; Zechariah 14:4

"And I saw the dead, small and great, stand before God; and the books were opened: and another book was opened, which is the book of life: and the dead were judged out of those things which were written in the books, according to their works.
And the sea gave up the dead which were in it; and death and hell delivered up the dead which were in them: and they were judged every man according to their works."
Revelation 20:12-13

Great White Throne

"And whosoever was not found written in the Book of Life was cast into the Lake of Fire."
Revelation 20:15

Resurrection of the Dead Unbelievers
Revelation 20:11-13; Jude 6

Unbelievers cast into Lake of Fire eternally

| About A.D. 30 | This Present Age | A.D.? Rapture | Seven Year Tribulation Period | Mount of Olives Armageddon | 1000 Year Millennial Age | With Satan Antichrist and False Prophet |

*Physical body remains in grave awaiting Rapture

Do Scriptures tell us how long the Marriage Supper will last?

Just as the official joining of a man to a woman is celebrated by a Marriage Supper, a banquet of rejoicing, so the union of Christ will have—reveal the scriptures—its banquet of rejoicing

Suggestions as to its length have varied from those who feel that it is a single festive meal at the start of the Millennium to those who liken it to a 1000 years of rejoicing with Christ during the entire Millennial Age. Some say it will be entirely in heaven, while the last half of the Tribulation is going on in the earth; but others have it as an affair on the earth.

The exact answer seems not to be revealed in Scripture in its details. Thus the venturing of opinions on such details becomes theoretical deduction at best. Such suggestions must be examined cautiously (not ridiculed—but examined). Suffice it to say that Scripture is crystal clear in revealing that there will be a grand and glorious supper celebrating Christ and the Church's forever being bodily together. All the redeemed will be there and it will be sometime after the Rapture (when at last Christ takes His Church to Himself). It will coincide with the joyous inauguration of the promised Kingdom of God.

What about those who have already gone to be with Christ . . . do they know what is going on here on earth

The wife of the president of a very fine theological seminary once declared that the answer to this must certainly be Yes. Her husband then assured her that the answer must be No. The truth is that we do not know for sure. Revelation 6:10, however, shows the early martyrs of the Tribulation Period asking the Lord.

"How long, O Lord, holy and true, dost thou not judge and avenge our blood on them that dwell on the earth?"

This shows that these in heaven have both an interest and a degree of knowledge concerning earthly happenings.

Will there be old and young in Heaven, according to the age at which they die? Or will all people in Heaven be the same age?

The Bible does not give an explicit answer on this. However in 1 Corinthians 15:42–44 we are told that the resurrection body will be different from our present body.

Our Present Body	Our Spiritual Body
Sown in corruption	Raised in Incorruption
Sown in dishonor	Raised in glory
Sown in weakness	Raised in power
Sown a natural body	Raised a spiritual body

These verses show clearly that we shall not carry any physical defects into Heaven.

Since all who go to Heaven will share in physical perfection it would appear that there will be no physical **"growing up"** in Heaven and thus no infants; but rather those who died as infants will have or soon come to have mature bodies. Likewise the aged will have what would be equal to a youthful, mature, vigorous body.

THREE HEAVENS

The word *heaven* is used hundreds of times in the Bible. The primary meaning of *heaven* is *"that which is above."* In God's Word *heaven* refers to one of three major realms as noted below.

THE HEAVENS	WHERE IS IT	SOME REFERENCES IN SCRIPTURE
THE ATMOSPHERIC HEAVENS	The atmosphere which surrounds the globe. Our troposphere is a blanket of air around earth. It is no higher than 20 miles above the earth. Most clouds are within 7 miles of the earth.	The Israelites were told that the land they were to possess "is a land of hills and valleys and drinketh water of the rain from heaven" (Deut. 11:11). See also Deut. 11:17, II Chron. 7:13, Isa. 55:9-11, Psalm 147:8, Matthew 24:30, Zach. 2:6.
THE CELESTIAL HEAVENS	This is the sphere in which the sun and moon and stars appear. I Kings 8:27 speaks of the Celestial Heavens when it says, "Behold, the heaven of heavens cannot contain God."	"And God said, Let there be lights in the firmament of the heaven to divide the day from the night..." (Genesis 1:14). "... Look now toward heaven, and tell the stars, if thou be able to number them..." (Genesis 15:5). See also Hebrews 1:10, Psalm 33:6, Isaiah 14:12, Amos 5:26 and Jeremiah 23:24.
THE BELIEVERS HEAVEN (The Abode of God)	This is characterized by holiness because God dwells there. Believers also will dwell in God's heaven because they have been made holy by the grace of God. Jesus assured us of the *reality* of this place (John 14:2).	"... I dwell in the high and holy place, with him also that is of a contrite and humble spirit..." (Isaiah 57:15). "Look down from heaven, and behold from the habitation of thy holiness and of thy glory ..." (Isaiah 63:15). See also Exodus 20:22, Deut. 4:36, Matthew 3:17, Matthew 14:19, Acts 7:55 and John 3:27.

Are there Scriptures that show that a believer goes to be with the Lord immediately after death

Yes. A number of Scriptures teach this.

You recall the Lord's words of assurance to the thief who turned to Him in faith on the cross:

"Today shalt thou be with Me in paradise" (Luke 23:43).
Read also our Lord's account of the rich man and Lazarus (Luke 16:22).

Another evidence is found in 2 Corinthians 5:6-8:

"Therefore we are always confident, knowing that, whilst we are at home in the body, we are absent from the Lord . . . we are . . . willing rather to be absent from the body, and to be present with the Lord."

These Scriptures indicate clearly that when a believer dies, he or she goes at once to be with the Lord. Absence from the body means presence with the Lord, how wonderful! This scripture alone refutes the false doctrine of soul sleep. For, if the dead in Christ remain unconscious in some long sleep of the soul until the resurrection, then Paul could *never* have said that he was *"willing rather to be absent from the body,"* that is, dead. Then it would be better for him to live as long as possible before the slumber of death. No, the moment a believer dies he or she is with their Lord. That is the Biblical teaching.

Will we be reunited with our loved ones in Heaven? Will we live again with our mates?

Scripture indicates that there will be no more separation in Heaven! All the saints of the ages will be there. No more will friends and loves ones have to part again. No more will families have to have tearful farewells (Revelation 21:4). What a grand reunion all saints in Christ will enjoy forever and forever (1 Thessalonians 4:15)!

In 1 Corinthians 15:44 we are told that in Heaven our bodies will be entirely different in nature. In Luke 20:35–36 the Lord tells us that the marriage relationship as we know it today has no place there, for there is no longer any need for the bearing of new children—death is no more and countless thousands and millions will be there who have been redeemed by Christ.

In 2 Corinthians 5:16, a key verse, we are told, *"Henceforth know we no man after the flesh; yea, though we have known Christ after the flesh, yet now henceforth know we Him no more."* This is saying that consequently, from now on we estimate and regard no one from a purely human point of view . . . even though we once estimated Christ from a human viewpoint. We shall know one another in Heaven and be able to rejoice together in the memories of God's grace to us.

The husband will recognize his wife and the wife her husband, and it will be a loving recognition . . . they will doubtless love one another as well as others in a lasting perfect love. All will be absorbed in the spiritual delights of their new condition in Christ.

There will be no need to carry photographs of loved ones in order to renew memories . . . for those Christians who have been absent for years will now be present in Heaven.

Thus, we will recognize our loved ones in Heaven but there is no Scripture which indicates we will live together as husband and wife precisely as we did on earth. Since Revelation 21:4 assures us of perfect bliss in the future world let no child of God be fearful. God made Heaven for us. He loves us, He knows our needs—it will not disappoint us. It will be wonderful, and there we shall at last be with Christ unseparated forever.

Does a believer who dies and goes to be with Christ recognize and know those who have gone before?

This appears to be so. Those with Jesus on the Mount of Transfiguration knew each other, even though they had never met Moses and Elijah (Matthew 17:1–8).

1 Corinthians 13:12 says *"Then shall I know, even as also I am known."* The word *know* here means *"to know fully."*

Our powers of perception, it would appear, will be enhanced and not diminished in Heaven.

REVELATION 22

20 He which testifieth these things saith, Surely I come quickly. Amen. Even so, come, Lord Jesus.

21 The grace of our Lord Jesus Christ *be* with you all. Amen.

Use this ORDER FORM to order additional copies of

QUESTIONS FREQUENTLY ASKED ME ON PROPHECY
by Salem Kirban

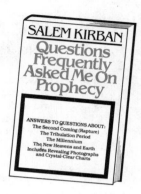

You will want to give **QUESTIONS FRE-QUENTLY ASKED ME ON PROPHECY** to loved ones and friends.

An excellent book to use as a study guide in Sunday School and fellowship groups. See bulk prices below.

PRICES

1 copy: $4.95

3 copies: $12 (You save $2.85)
5 copies: $20 (You save $4.74)
10 copies or more: $3 per copy

- -

ORDER FORM

Salem Kirban, Inc.
Kent Road
Huntingdon Valley, Pennsylvania 19006

Enclosed find $ _____ for _____ copies of
QUESTIONS FREQUENTLY ASKED ME ON PROPHECY by Salem Kirban.
*I will pay UPS for small delivery charge.

Name_____
  Mr./Mrs./Miss   (Please PRINT)

Street_____

City_____

State_____Zip Code_____

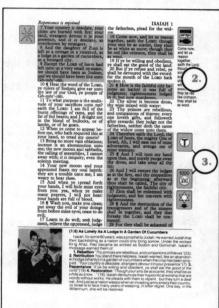

4. Rare, Old Bible Etchings

Unusual etchings of Bible scenes designed by craftsmen over 100 years ago. Enjoy the same etchings your great grandparents found joy and comfort in!

5. Full Color Holy Land Photographs

Vivid photographs taken by Salem Kirban reveal the beauty of the Promised Land as it is **right now** . . . today!

6. Full Color Charts on Future Events

Over 50 Charts including the 21 Tribulation Judgments, Three Coming Decisive Wars, The Three Heavens, The Resurrections. A few are picture below in reduced size.

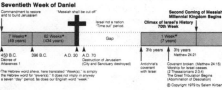

Time Period Views of The Prophets
The prophets had a twofold ministry. They exposed the sins of their own time. They also revealed the future (as God revealed it to them).

When reading the Books written by the 16 prophets (Isaiah through Malachi) this Chart will help you understand the scope of time periods referred to by the prophet.

© Copyright 1979 by Salem Kirban

Seventieth Week of Daniel

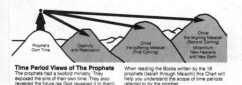

Bible History and Prophecy Through The Ages

© Copyright 1979 by Salem Kirban

7. 380 Page Commentary on The Book of REVELATION

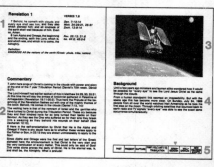

The last book in the Bible, **Revelation,** deals with future events and is the most difficult book for many to understand. We have Visualized the book by **1** placing only 2 verses on each page **2** writing a clear Commentary **3** including an explanatory illustration **4** tying the verses in to current events and **5** by a red arrow, pointing to the proper Time Period!

8. Major Doctrines Explained

There are at least 28 major Doctrines in the Bible. These DOCTRINES are explained in Commentary units marked with this Symbol placed next to identifying verse!

9. Major Attributes Explained

There are 17 Attributes *(or characteristics)* that identify God! Each ATTRIBUTE is explained in Commentary units marked with this Symbol placed next to identifying verse!

10. Extra NEW TESTAMENT Commentary

As an added bonus, you will discover **100 added pages** of special New Testament Commentary. All in FULL COLOR. Includes many Charts, Maps and Graphs!

HOW TO LIVE ABOVE AND
BEYOND YOUR CIRCUMSTANCES
by Salem Kirban $4.95

At last! Here are practical answers to perplexing problems that face Christians everyday. Answers to almost 50 questions that face young people, those who are married and those in the Golden Years of life. Full color! Over 100 photos!

LEBANON . . . A HARVEST OF LOVE
by Layyah A. Barakat
Photo Commentary by Salem Kirban $3.95

This unforgettable true story of how a barefoot girl from Lebanon overcame insurmountable odds to reach her people for Christ. A classic missionary story of trials, testings and final triumph! Full color photographs!

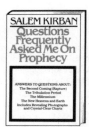

QUESTIONS FREQUENTLY
ASKED ME ON PROPHECY
by Salem Kirban $4.95

This new updated version of a popular best-seller will answer those difficult questions many people sidestep. Answers clearly given to questions on Bible prophecy. Includes revealing photographs and crystal clear charts. **Plus added features!**

REVELATION VISUALIZED
by Gary G. Cohen
and Salem Kirban $12.75

Enlarged and updated. Excellent for teaching or studying Revelation. Only two verses to a page. Balance of page is explanatory commentary plus charts and photographs. Full Color! **Each verse has Red Arrow pointing to specific Time Period!**

THE RISE OF ANTICHRIST
by Salem Kirban $4.95

While the church sleeps . . . the advance forces of Antichrist have already arrived! Over 20 chapters include: *The Day They Reshape Man, The Plan To Control the Human Mind, The Day They Transplant Memories* . . . plus much more. Filled with PHOTOS!

SATAN'S ANGELS EXPOSED
by Salem Kirban $4.95

At last! Satan's strategy is revealed! Most people are unaware that Satan's subtle deception has now infiltrated the Christian church. Special section shows how secret organizations (like the **Illuminati**) operate to control the world! Illustrated!

SATAN'S MUSIC EXPOSED
by Lowell Hart
Photo Commentary by Salem Kirban $4.95

Lowell Hart was a former band leader. Now as a music instructor at Prairie Bible Institute he reveals how the contemporary sounds making inroads into the Church are part of Satan's plan to water down its effectiveness. Well illustrated!

666/1000
by Salem Kirban $5.95

New! A Double Volume! 480 pages! Two Bestsellers combined into One complete volume! **666** is a novel which vividly captures events as they may occur during the Tribulation. **1000** is a sequel which takes the same cast of characters through the Millennium!

666 (Pictorial Format)
by Salem Kirban $2.95

The entire book, **666,** has been transformed into a **FULL COLOR Pictorial Format.** This 64 page Quality Paperback is excellent for young and old alike. It pictorially describes the Tribulation Period and how the forces of Antichrist operate!

YOUR LAST GOODBYE
by Salem Kirban $4.95

This book tells you all about HEAVEN! It also reveals in clear, easy to understand language exactly what happens **THE MOMENT YOU DIE!** Over 65 charts and photos. Full Color. Over 300 pages! A book with rare information!

SALEM KIRBAN HEALTH BOOKS

Salem Kirban has spoken on Bible Prophecy in over 300 churches. Many times people, who were obviously ill, came to him asking for prayer. It was then Salem realized that he should write a few books on the Biblical approach to sound nutritional health!

HOW JUICES RESTORE HEALTH NATURALLY
by Salem Kirban $4.95

Salem Kirban reveals how he found the Fountain of Youth **at age 50!** He tells his own experiences of how juices eliminated fatigue . . . gave him new vitality . . . a new lease on life. **Fourteen** different juice combinations illustrated in **FULL COLOR!**

HOW TO EAT YOUR WAY BACK TO VIBRANT HEALTH
by Salem Kirban $4.95

Includes **147** different health restoring meals plus a special **3-Day Turn Around Diet!** Answers given to many questions people often ask about what foods to eat, how to have Reserve Energy, how to turn your marriage into a honeymoon!

HOW TO KEEP HEALTHY AND HAPPY BY FASTING
by Salem Kirban $4.95

A best-selling book on Fasting that approaches the subject Biblically! Discover the secret of how fasting relieves tension, helps you sleep better, restores your energy level eliminating fatigue. Plus much more! Filled with photographs!

THE GETTING BACK TO NATURE DIET
by Salem Kirban $4.95

Salem Kirban's best and most complete book on Health. Revealed at last! Nature's Secrets for keeping you well! **Only found in this book . . .** the most comprehensive Food Charts showing both **HIGH Stress** and **Low Stress** foods. Excellent!

Quantity	Description	Price	Total
_____	Charts On Revelation	$ 4.95	_____
_____	Countdown To Rapture	4.95	_____
_____	Guide To Survival	4.95	_____
_____	How To Be Sure Of Crowns In Heaven	4.95	_____
_____	How To Live Above Your Circumstances	4.95	_____
_____	Lebanon . . . A Harvest Of Love	3.95	_____
_____	Questions Frequently Asked Me On Prophecy	4.95	_____
_____	Revelation Visualized (September, 1980)	12.75	_____
_____	Satan's Angels Exposed	4.95	_____
_____	Satan's Music Exposed	4.95	_____
_____	666/1000	5.95	_____
_____	666 PICTORIAL FORMAT	2.95	_____
_____	The Rise Of Antichrist	4.95	_____
_____	Your Last Goodbye	4.95	_____
_____	Armstrong's Church Of God (Plain Truth)	4.95	_____
_____	Jehovah's Witnesses	4.95	_____
_____	Mormonism	4.95	_____
_____	Christian Science	4.95	_____
_____	How Juices Restore Health Naturally	4.95	_____
_____	How To Eat Your Way To Vibrant Health	4.95	_____
_____	How To Keep Healthy By Fasting	4.95	_____
_____	The Getting Back To Nature Diet	4.95	_____
_____	The Salem Kirban REFERENCE BIBLE	47.77	_____

Total for Books _____

Shipping & Handling _____

Total Enclosed $ _____

(We do NOT invoice. Check must accompany order, please.)

☐ Check enclosed.
☐ Master Charge
☐ VISA

When using Credit Card, show number in space below.

When Using Master Charge
Also Give Interbank
No. (Just above your
name on card)

Card Expires	Month	Year

POSTAGE & HANDLING Use this easy chart to figure postage, shipping and handling charges. Send correct amount and avoid delay.

TOTAL FOR BOOKS	Up to 5.00	5.01-10.00	10.01-20.00	20.01-35.00	Over 35.00
DELIVERY CHARGE	1.50	2.00	2.50	2.95	NO CHARGE

FOR ADDITIONAL SAVINGS: Orders Over $35.00 Are Now Postage-Free!

SHIP TO_____

Mr./Mrs./Miss   (Please PRINT)

Address_____

City_____State_____ZIP_____

SALEM KIRBAN, Inc., Kent Rd., Huntingdon Valley, Pa. 19006